P9-CSB-573

YESH!

MUTTS IV
by.
· PATRICK McDONNELL ·

**Andrews McMeel
Publishing**

Kansas City

Mutts is distributed internationally by King Features Syndicate, Inc. For information write King Features Syndicate, Inc., 235 East 45th Street, New York, New York 10017.

Yesh! Mutts IV copyright © 1999 by Patrick McDonnell. All rights reserved. Printed in the United States of America. No part of this book may be used or reproduced in any manner whatsoever without written permission except in the case of reprints in the context of reviews. For information write Andrews McMeel Publishing, an Andrews McMeel Universal company, 4520 Main Street, Kansas City, Missouri 64111.

www.andrewsmcmeel.com

00 01 02 03 BAH 10 9 8 7 6 5 4 3

ISBN: 0-8362-8286-8

Library of Congress Catalog Card Number: 98-88673

Yesh! Is printed on recycled paper.

5

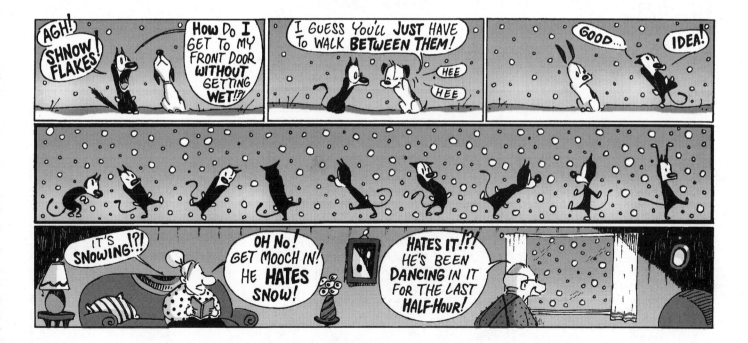

8

9

11

12

OLD MOTHER HUBBARD WENT TO THE CUPBOARD TO GET HER DOG A BONE
BUT WHEN SHE GOT THERE THE CUPBOARD WAS BARE AND SO THE POOR DOG HAD...

21

MUTTS.

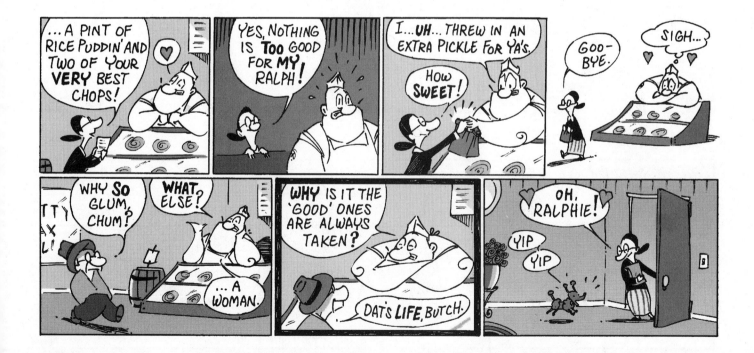

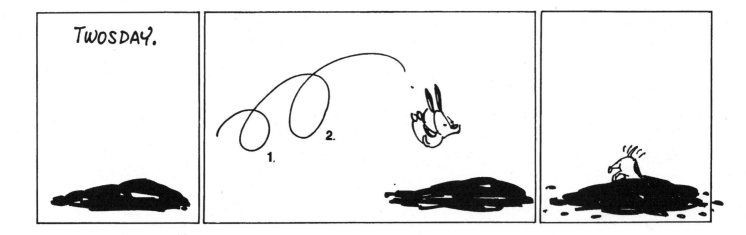

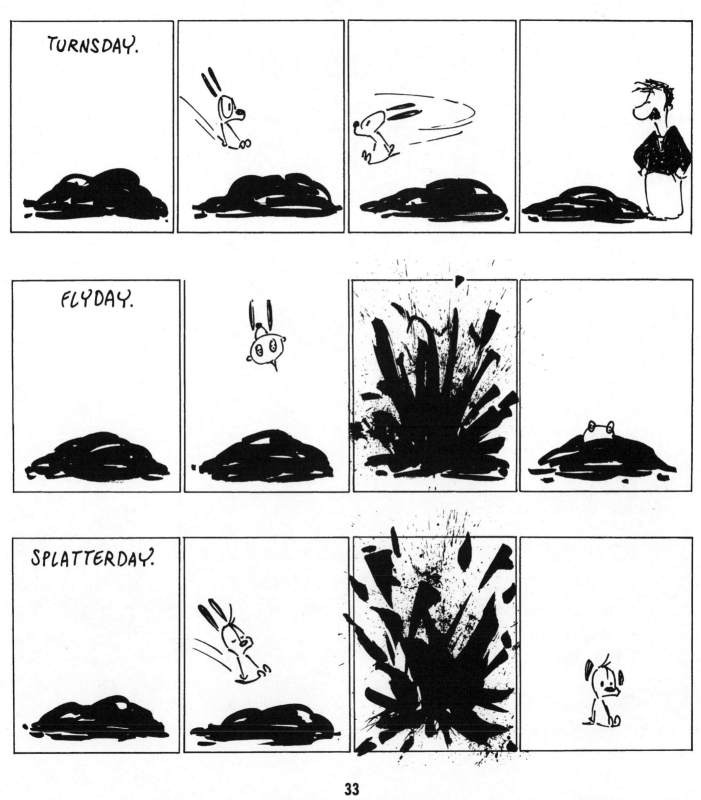

39

MUTS

by
· PATRICK McDONNELL ·

50

Panel 1: AHHH... THE GRASS IS **SO** SHOFT. THIS FIELD IS GREAT!
EXCEPT FOR **THAT** ORGAN MUSIC...

Panel 2: MMMM... I SHMELL HOT DOGS!
...AND PEANUTS!

Panel 3: **WHAT** THE HECK IS THAT!?!

Panel 4: THAT'S A NASTY SWARM OF BUGS.
YETH.

Panel 5: WHAT ARE YOU EATING?
OH, JUST A LI'L...

Panel 6: ...FISH.

58

61

MUTTS.

· bY PATRICK McDONNELL ·

73

74

MUTTS
by
Patrick
McDonnell

It's **OUR** ANNIVERSARY.

SHTUCK AGAIN.

GROWWL...

OH PO'PO' TUMMY— MY LI'L CHUMMY.

ALL I CAN THINK ABOUT IS EATING.

YOU LOOKED HUNGRY, SO I BROUGHT YOU A WORM.

AWESOME!

NOW I DON'T FEEL LIKE EATING AT ALL!

GROOVY!

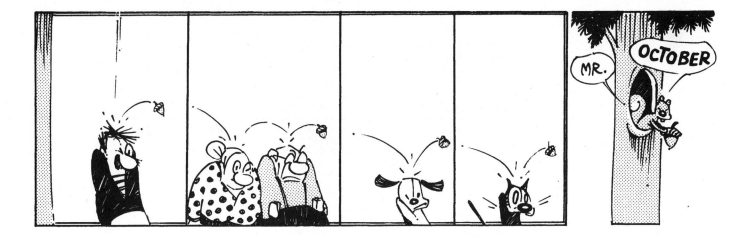

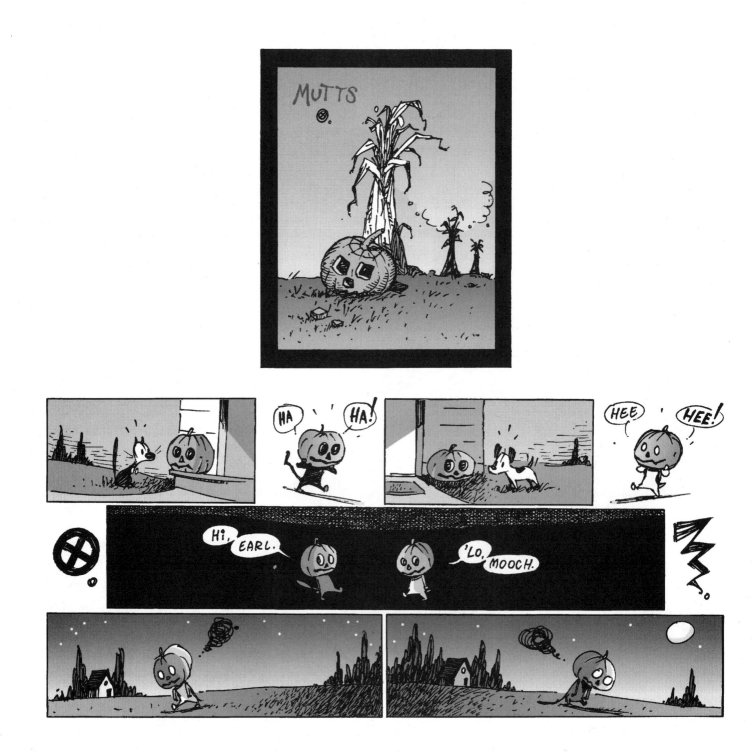

105

117

MUTTS.

— P.M.